LUMINOUS VECTORS

RUDRA PRATAP SINGH

Made with ♥ on the Notion Press Platform
www.notionpress.com

LUMINOUS VECTORS

I would like to extend my heartfelt gratitude to my father, Dr. Hare Ram Sing, and my mother, Jagriti Devi, without whose unwavering support this book would not have been possible.

Contents

DISCLAIMER *ix*

About the author *xi*

Preface *xiii*

1. BE YOU 1
2. FORGIVENESS 2
3. DISTRACTION 4
4. YOUTHS 7
5. PEOPLE 8
6. MYSTERY 11
7. OPPPORTUNITY 12
8. LISTENING 14
9. TOLERANCE 15
10. DETERMINED 17
11. SUCCESS 18
12. IDENTIFYING 19
13. MISTAKE 22
14. WHY PATIENCE 23
15. LIFE 24
16. PATIENCE 25
17. LEADER 28
18. Women Safety 29

HUMANS

TIME

WORDS

Contents

19. HUMANS, TIME AND WORDS 37

20. BUSY 39

21. WHY YOU? 40

22. CONCLUSION 42

LUMINOUS VECTORS

Disclaimer

The information contained in this book represents my personal opinions and experiences based on my observations and reflections throughout my life. While I have tried my best to make it accurate. Therefore, it is important to recognize that my perspectives are subjective and may not be applicable to everyone. Readers are advised to seek information and consider it if they want.

About The Author

Rudra is a dynamic 16-year-old currently navigating the challenges and excitement of Standard 11 while pursuing his passion for science. Beyond his academic pursuit, he is interested in public speaking. His enthusiasm extends to social work and aspiring to dedicate his future to women's safety.

Rudra Pratap Singh

Preface

Success is a journey, not a destination, and it often unfolds through a series of deliberate steps and profound insights. In a world brimming with self-help advice and success strategies, it can be challenging to discern which paths are most effective.

Drawing from a blend of personal experiences, timeless wisdom, and contemporary strategies, each line explores a key approach to attaining success.

Understanding the things mentioned in the book would guide you to a bright path, which will not only help to make you successful but will also make you a good human being. It would help you to live a healthy life, have healthy relationships, and create a positive impact on society.

As you delve into this book, you will find that success is not merely about reaching a particular milestone but about cultivating habits, mindsets, and practices that foster growth and resilience.

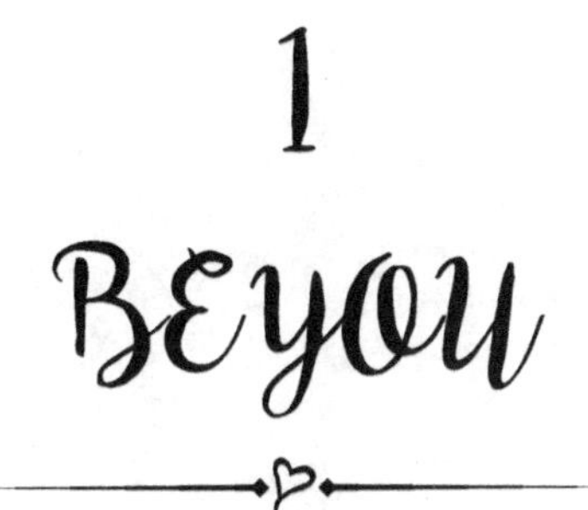

FOCUS ON "YOU" , NOT OTHERS.

COMPETE WITH YOURSELF NOT WITH OTHERS.

REMEMBER YOU ARE THE MAIN CHARACTER OF YOUR LIFE.

2

FORGIVENESS

People often misunderstand the meaning of forgiveness, believing that forgiveness means accepting or excusing the wrong action rather than acknowledging it and choosing to move beyond it. Not just this, but forgiveness is sometimes also misunderstood by forgetting the incident. There is a very famous quote, "Forgive but never forget," which means to let go of the anger or resentment associated with a hurtful experience while still remembering the lesson or impact of the event.

Keeping any kind of emotional burden, grudges, resentment, or carrying negative emotion hinders a person's ability to make decisions. Forgiveness can alleviate these emotional weights, leading to a free mind and clearer thinking, which would eventually improve focus. Mental clarity is very important for setting up and achieving goals, as it allows individuals to use their energy in some productive activities rather than being consumed by past grievances. Forgiveness plays a key role in maintaining and rebuilding trust, which is fundamental for effective collaboration and networking. By addressing conflict and forgiving the past, one can develop a very strong relationship, which would foster growth. Apart from this, forgiveness also helps an individual by encouraging empathy and inclusivity and inspiring positive change.

If a person does not know how to forgive, they may face several negative effects in their life, impacting their emotional, psychological, and social well-being. We often see individuals who hold grudges, are short-tempered, suffer from stress and anxiety, or have a strained relationship. All this holds an individual back, creates a negative impact on self-esteem, and leads to isolation and eventually overall life satisfaction. Hence, forgiveness is very important for personal growth. And we often hear that a person who says they are sorry is strong, but the person who forgives is the strongest.

3

DISTRACTION

DISTRACTION IS NOT DUE TO LACK OF FOCUS, BUT DUE TO OVERSTIMULATION.

Focusing on something is difficult if your mind is overexcited about something. We often hear from our elders that a child's mind is like a sponge, soaking up information and adapting everything that they see around them; hence, overstimulation is very common in children. When their mind is overwhelmed by various distractions and excitements, focusing on their studies become challenging. The constant pull of outdoor activities with friends, the excitement of video games, the endless content on social media, or the anticipation of upcoming events can make it even harder for them to concentrate. This flood of competing interests and stimuli scatters their attention, making it difficult to engage deeply with their schoolwork. Their thoughts are pulled in many directions, preventing them from maintaining the focused mental effort needed to study effectively. Not just children, but in today's fast-moving world, every individual wants to be successful, wants respect in their society, wants respect at their workplace, and, for all this, they seek growth in their professional life, but this is not possible without proper management of stimulation.

Not just most of the research but also my personal experience indicates that after spending the entire day distracted, many people often find themselves reflecting at night on their desire for success and resolving to make a change the next day. But again, on the next day, they repeat their mistake, wasting time on social media, partying late at night with friends, consuming unhealthy junk food, and engaging in other diversions. And I don't blame them for this, because most people are not even aware of what distraction is. Why is it caused? What is overstimulation?

Overstimulation is very dangerous. It not only causes distraction, but it could kill a healthy individual from inside and can kill inner identity or core self. I have seen someone getting killed day by day because of overstimulation. The way it promotes stress, mental fatigue, emotional irritability, sleep disturbances, decreased quality of relationships, impaired cognitive function, increased anxiety, and burnout makes a person feel hollow, as if they've become dead from the inside. Gaining control over overstimulation will not only help an individual stay focused but will also fulfill their desires. One can obtain control over overstimulation by identifying triggers and paying attention to what causes overstimulation, whether it is certain people, environments, activities, or any social interaction. Engage in relaxing activities, discover yourself, find activities that make you feel good, and unwind, such as listening to music, reading books, talking to people, and spending time with friends or nature. Practice self-awareness, regularly check in with yourself to assess your level of stimulation, and adjust your activities accordingly. Set boundaries. Limit your exposure to overstimulating activities or environments. This might mean setting specific times for work and rest or taking breaks between tasks.

Sometimes noise is a very important factor. Identify what kind of noise disturbs you, or you can even use noise cancellation tools.

4

YOUTHS

REMEMBER WE YOUTHS ARE THE FUTURE ASSETS.

PEOPLE

DON'T THINK ABOUT WHAT OTHERS THINK ABOUT YOU.

THEIR THOUGHT IS THEIR BUSINESS, NOT YOURS.

From where I see the world I have always seen people worrying about what others think about them. It is said that different people have different opinions, there are approximately 8.2 billion people in the world as of 2024 and every individual may have different opinions. So just think what you will do if all these people will come to you and give their opinion on you, is it possible to do something that everyone will like?

No, it is not, so do things that you feel are good for you. Others' perceptions are merely reflections of their own experiences and biases, and they don't define your true worth. What's most important is having a strong belief in yourself, staying true to yourself and your own values. Even in my life, I used to think of what others would think about me which made me very under confident. Every time I undertook a task, my mind would incessantly send me the message, 'What will others think of you if you do this?', constantly plagued by a relentless preoccupation with others' judgments and perceptions. Your sense of self should come from within, not be influenced by external judgments. Focus on what makes you feel authentic and fulfilled.

We are all humans, and humans seek validation from others but what is important is having a true belief in oneself. We all have or will meet people in our life who will try creating, negative aura around us, after all not everyone is good on this planet. People would be jealous of you and in their jealousy, they would come to you, behaving like they are your friends, and in their jealousy, they will give you Faulty Guidance or Erroneous advice. And when you meet these kinds of fellows, remember, they are acting out of jealousy or ill intent and offer you erroneous advice, it's important to navigate the situation carefully. And I strongly believe that if people are jealous of you then you are on the track of success. **It is not easy to distinguish between helpful guidance and harmful manipulation.** Even in my life, many individuals came to me pretending as if they were my well-wishers with the intent of offering misguided advice to undermine my success. And yes, I was trapped in it. However, with time and reflection, I came to realize the true nature of their actions. Slowly and gradually, I learned to critically assess advice and to trust in my own judgment, recognizing that not everyone who offers guidance has a good intent or is your well-wisher. This experience taught me valuable lessons about discernment and the importance of surrounding myself with genuine support.

And I firmly believe that once a person stops worrying about others' negative judgments and focuses solely on their own. Then no one could stop them from unlocking their true potential. It's very difficult to ignore external pressure but if one does it, it allows one to focus on personal goals and aspirations, free from the constraints of societal expectations. And yes, when you let go of the need for validation from others and instead trust in your own vision, you open the door to reach new heights and be successful in life.

LIFE IS A MYSTERY, KEEP SOLVING IT.

7

OPPPORTUNITY

GRAB EVERY OPPPORTUNITY

Never let go of anything if it is in your hand; give your best till the last movement.

Regert

We often regret our decisions; we think about the opportunities we should have seized or the paths we should have stayed on; sometimes we even replay the scenarios in our mind and wish that we acted differently. And it gets very difficult to let go of this regret; sometimes it even stays with us for life. I am not talking about any particular field here like losing someone, getting bad grades, or missing a prize by a small margin, but I am talking about a wider field that includes all these things and even more.

A Pathway to Success

In the journey of life, opportunities are the stepping stones that paves growth not only in personal but also in professional life. Seizing every opportunity that comes our way is very important because it helps us to achieve personal development and goals. Opportunities often come in various forms—some as grand milestones, others as simple, everyday chances for improvement. It is strongly believed that life is a race, and hence opportunities will not wait for us; we will have to grab them every time they are in our hands.

Inspiring others

Embracing or grabbing opportunity is not only about personal gain, but it is also about creating a positive impact on others. If you take up new challenges and make it a success, people around you would be inspired. They would think, “If he can, why can’t” we?

And hence it would not only inspire people to do good things but also help in creating a good society. Your willingness to step up can open doors for others and foster an environment of growth and possibility.

Grab every opportunity that you get. This line is really special as well as powerful for me, as my teacher always said this to me. Grabging every opportunity that comes your way is a vital aspect of achieving success and personal fulfillment. It not only helps us to create an impact on society and inspire others but also provides a pathway to success for an individual in both personal and professional life and keeps us away from any future regret.

8

LISTENING

ANYONE CAN SPEAK BUT NOT EVERYONE CAN LISTEN.

9

TOLERANCE

TOLERANCE IS NOT ABOUT IGNORING OR MERELY ENDURING DIFFERENCE, BUT ABILITY OR WILLINGNESS TO ACCEPT AND RESPECT DIFFERENCE

Accepting difference, whether in terms of belief, opinion, or behavior, is tolerance. To be successful, a person must have the ability to do so; the person must value the coexistence of various perspectives and lifestyles, even if the perspective is different from one's own. When one thinks about tolerance, they just equate it with simply putting up with something or someone; they don't accept the diversity. The word tolerance indeed is something very big as well as powerful. In other words, tolerance can be explained as an open-minded approach, the ability of a person to accept as well as respect another person's belief or opinion, even if it is different from oneself. I have seen many people say that I am a very tolerant person, but they are unaware of true tolerance.

True tolerance requires empathy and a willingness to understand others' viewpoints, even when they conflict with our own. For which a person must have a good listening skill (all seven listening skills). By fostering an environment where different/diverse voices are heard and respected, we can collaborate and solve many of the challenging problems in the world. Which would eventually lead to personal as well as professional development of an individual.

We have also seen in our history how intolerance led to conflict, division, and, moreover, destruction. And that destruction set us back by many years, impeding our progress and delaying our development. It is also important to mention that tolerance doesn't mean compromising one's own thoughts or opinions but instead accepting others opinions that they hold. Tolerance fosters a respectful dialogue where individuals can discuss and debate differing opinions without hostility.

Now the most important thing is that tolerance is very essential at workplaces, as it helps us to create a good relationship with our colleagues, seniors, managers, or boss. One of the primary ways tolerances contribute to success is through the enrichment of interpersonal relationships. In such a diverse world, there are people with different opinions, beliefs, and behaviors. Tolerance helps individuals to deal with all kinds of people, understand them, and eventually resolve any kind of conflict and build a strong and respectful partnership. By fostering strong interpersonal relationships, encouraging personal growth, navigating diverse professional environments, and building a positive reputation, tolerance becomes a powerful tool for success.

10

DETERMINED

BE DETERMINED FOR SUCCESS TO COME.

11

Success

BE SUCCESSFUL WITH GLORY.

BE SUCCESSFUL BUT DON'T HARM SOMEONE FOR THAT.

12

IDENTIFYING

Identifying means recognizing, determining, or establishing something's nature or identity.

Identifying indeed is a big topic to discuss, but there are few things that one should identify to achieve their goals and be successful, and we would be discussing only those things. Living life without a true well-wisher can be incredibly challenging. In times of struggle, having someone who genuinely supports and believes in you makes a significant difference. Identifying your real friends, your well-wishers, is very important, as they always stand by you, giving emotional strength to an individual.

Without such a person, life becomes very difficult and overwhelming. They guide us in our tough times; their opinions and advice help a person to grow in life. Building and nurturing these relationships can lead to a more fulfilling and successful life. It is strongly believed that if a person is happy in his life, he can do anything in the world as he knows his true value and potential. Therefore, having a friend who is always there for you is invaluable in achieving your goals and finding happiness. Another important thing is identifying your goal. Identifying your goal is a fundamental step toward achieving fulfillment and success in life. It serves as a compass that directs your efforts and resources, providing clarity and purpose. If a person is not clear with his goal, distraction would automatically come. A distracted person would constantly change his aspiration by seeing others, eventually falling into a trap and achieving nothing due to their inability to commit to a single goal. Persistence plays a vital role in identifying your goal. It is a crucial attribute in the journey toward achieving your goals. Challenges and obstacles are inevitable, but a determined attitude can help you overcome them. Embrace failures as learning opportunities and use them to refine your approach. Adaptability is also essential; as you progress, you may need to reassess and adjust your goals to reflect new insights or changes in circumstances. Flexibility ensures that your goals remain relevant and achievable as you grow and evolve.

Identifying and pursuing your goals is a transformative process that requires introspection, strategic planning, and persistent effort. By understanding what truly matters to you and setting clear, actionable objectives, you can navigate your path to success with purpose and determination. The journey of goal-setting not only leads to personal and professional growth but also fosters a deeper sense of fulfillment. Once you have a clear vision of what you want to achieve, the next step is to set some smart goals. A smart goal is specific, measurable, achievable, relevant, and time-bound; it is specific and clear; rather than saying, "I want to get fit," say, "I will be working out 2 hours a day." Ultimately, the effort invested in identifying and achieving your goals is a powerful way to shape your future and lead a meaningful life.

Weakness and strength are the two magical words. As they encapsulate the dual aspects of human experience, representing both the vulnerabilities and the potentials within us. If a person is very clear and aware of both his strengths and weaknesses, then he is a step closer to success. Being aware of one's weakness makes the person prepare for the future; a self-aware person has more powers and tactics to deal in a challenging situation. Being aware of one's weakness can help a person to work on it and convert its weakness into his strength. Recognizing one's strength would make a person even more confident, making you more prepared to tackle tasks with assurance. Like if a situation arises to complete a task within their area of expertise, an individual can approach it with assurance, resulting in not only successful completion but also a higher quality outcome.

LEARN FROM YOUR MISTAKE, DON'T BE SHAMEFUL OF IT.

14

WHY PATIENCE

LIFE IS NOT SAME FOR EVERYONE BUT WITH PATIENCE YOU CAN MAKE IT.

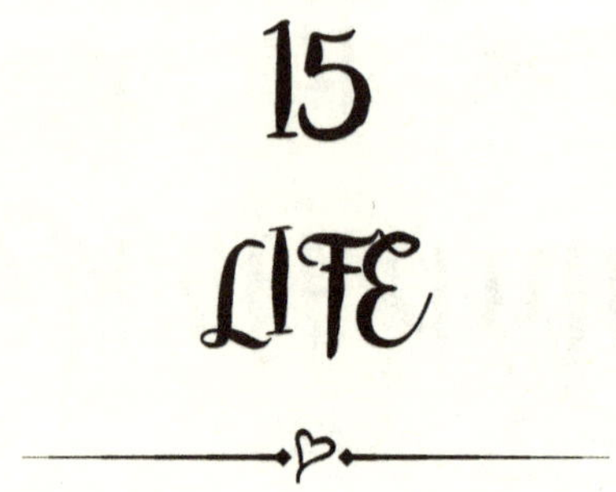

LIVE LIFE TO THE FULLEST, BECAUSE HUMANS ARE MORTAL.

PATIENCE IS NOT THE ABILITY TO WAIT WITHOUT COMPLAINT.

Patience encompasses much more—it involves a proactive and resilient mindset that helps individuals navigate challenges with composure and persistence. There will be times when your hard work will not show instant results; that is the time when we need true patience. It is not about passively enduring delays or hardships, but about actively maintaining a positive attitude and making thoughtful decisions even when immediate results are not apparent.

Growth and success are seldom effortless, but with patience, the arduous journey transforms into a navigable path, making the pursuit more manageable and ultimately more attainable. I have a strong belief that patience provides us with everything we need, and I am saying this through my personal experience. Whenever we look for pursuing academic excellence, career advancement, or personal development, all these things often require enduring periods of struggle and delay. An individual who does not have patience loses hope and moves on in life, but later, when he looks back, he is filled with regrets and 'what if'. Doing nothing is very easy; just think about it: is it really easy to do nothing?

While doing nothing may seem easy, maintaining patience often proves challenging because it requires us to confront our own impatience and discomfort, reminding us that true patience is not merely waiting but enduring with a positive mindset. Life is a journey marked by its ups and downs, where each moment unfolds at its own pace. We often find ourselves being desperate about our result or something else, but we forget that true progress requires time. Patience helps us navigate life's uncertainties with grace and resilience. Rather than rushing through challenges, patience teaches us to appreciate the journey and trust in the eventual outcome. In professional life, there would be times when your thoughts would not match with your colleagues, manager, or boss, but you will have to be tolerant as well as patient. And that is why we need to understand the importance of patience in this journey of life.

BE A LEADER.

A LEADER ALWAYS ASK 'WHAT CAN I DO FOR YOU?'

18

Women safety

As we navigate the **luminous vectors** that guide us towards success and fulfillment, there is also a matter that needs to be brought to our attention as a society as it is in accordance with our principles: women's safety. While this attempt focuses on the lights and routes on personal accomplishment and the creation of good, we cannot avoid that safety is the first rule for fulfilling these purposes.

In the modern world, whether it is success in personal achievements or social aspirations, it cannot be realized without the safety and wellbeing of one's self. It is not a side issue since women's safety is a necessary condition upon which we skillfully work to survive. Whenever safety is treated lightly, it clouds the bright pathways that we are trying to brighten up.

In this sense, it is in this pursuit of an enlightened way of life that immersing oneself in the protection of women emerges. It shows staunch dedication towards underprivileged members of society, particularly the female gender, that dictates the establishment of safe environments so that individuals can go forward and achieve their ideals without fear. Safeguarding is just as fundamental as these vectors, which take space and time and aim towards clarification and success.

This integration of this knowledge profoundly distinguishes our journey as we appreciate the linkage of personal and societal wellness. Thus, when we stand for safety, we amplify the very factors that result in a successful and meaningful life.

Moreover, dealing with women's safety helps in expanding the understanding of what it is to live a life worth living. It reinforces the fact that success and health are not independent goals but rather are interdependent with the rest of society. A protective and just society increases the ability for individual development as well as the ability for creating change within society, making it more worthwhile and useful to seek ways to make those who strive to illuminate ways.

In this vein, let us be consultative and hands-on, so that those resplendent paths we follow in his work may also be for self-advancement, but also for the pledge to create an equitable society. We thus respect the nature of that journey and bring about a situation where all can walk their own paths towards success, those paths well lit by the presence of safety and opportunity.

At last, the process of self-reaching complex and multiple success not only becomes the guest of all but rather becomes the symbol and example of how personal progress can be complemented by the quest for a safe and just world. Hence, as we tread upon how to advance these, let us be focused on the safety of the people, for it is through focused people that the way to everyone together in one society would become brighter and better.

HUMANS

HUMANS ARE MORTAL.

TIME

TIME DOES NOT WAIT FOR ANYONE OR ANYTHING.

WORDS

BE CAREFUL WITH YOUR WORDS.

19

HUMANS, TIME AND WORDS

We have already discussed the seven ways to success, but there are a few more things that are important in the journey of life. These things will not only help you to be successful but will also help you to maintain a healthy lifestyle, healthy relationships, create a positive impact on society, and yes, the positive aura that would be created around you after achieving all these things will attract people around you. Time does not wait for anyone or anything. I have witnessed people weeping over the loss of someone, even though they know those who are gone will not return. I don't blame them for this, their grief; it's a natural response to loss. But we should always remember that time moves on regardless of our sorrow. We must prepare ourselves and teach our minds that human mortality is a fundamental truth. Accepting our own impermanence allows us to cherish each moment and live more meaningfully. If we value the time, it will, in return, value us by rewarding our efforts and respecting our commitment. Moving on to the third thing, which is being careful about your words. There was a time in my life when I didn't even give a second thought before saying anything to anyone. But now I have realized how stupid I was, and now I am aware of the power of the words. We can never truly know which words might hurt someone, the potential consequences, or how emotionally or mentally resilient they are. I have come to know the profound impact words can have. Each person's capacity to handle words varies, and what might seem insignificant to one could be deeply damaging to another.

20
Busy

ALWAYS KEEP YOUR MIND INVOLVED IN SOMETHING

21

Why You?

Give time to yourself. In today's fast-paced world, our lives have become increasingly hectic, with endless to-do lists and constant demands on our time. This leads to frequent fatigue and burnout. If we do not do anything about this, the fatigue will be converted into a chronic one. Amidst the rush and the noise, giving yourself a moment to pause and reflect can make a significant difference. It's essential to carve out a few quiet minutes before you go to bed to look back on your day. Therefore, I suggest taking out five minutes of your day before going to bed, analyzing what you did the whole day, whether you were productive or not, what were the things that made you happy, identifying people who infused your day with positivity, and identifying the things that you wanted to do but couldn't. Doing all these things will have a powerful benefit. This brief period of introspection can enhance your self-awareness, improve your time management, and boost your overall well-being.

So, amidst the chaos of daily life, remember to give yourself these precious moments of introspection. It's a small investment in your health and happiness that can lead to more balanced and fulfilling days ahead.

22
Conclusion

#01

Stay focused.

#02

Don't let other people's words affect you.

#03

Learn to grab opportunities.

#04

Value other people's opinions.

#05

Appreciate people.

#06

Set smart goals, identify your strengths and weaknesses.

#07

Control your emotions.

www.ingramcontent.com/pod-product-compliance
Lightning Source LLC
La Vergne TN
LVHW091237150826
845673LV00003B/1176

* 9 7 9 8 8 9 5 5 6 6 7 1 8 *